DAY OF THE DEAD
A Mexican-American Celebration

Library of Congress Cataloging-in-Publication Data

Hoyt-Goldsmith, Diane.
    Day of the dead : a Mexican-American celebration / Diane Hoyt
-Goldsmith ; photographs by Lawrence Migdale. – 1st ed.
      p.   cm.
    "Age level: 8-12; grade level: 4-6" – CIP data sheet.
    Includes index.
    ISBN 0-8234-1094-3
    1. All Souls' Day – Mexico – Juvenile literature.   2. Mexico – Social
life and customs – Juvenile literature.   [1. All Souls' Day.
2. Mexican Americans – Social life and customs.   3. Fasts and feasts –
Mexico.]   I. Migdale, Lawrence, II.   II. Title.
GT4995.A4H69   1994
394.2'64 – dc20   93-42106
                                                                                      CIP
                                                                                      AC

Acknowledgments

In creating this book, we enjoyed the cooperation and enthusiasm of many
people. We would like to express our appreciation to the Cid family —
Armando, Josefina, Zenaida, Armando, Azucena, Ximena, and Miguel.
We also thank the grandparents, Clara and Manuel Cid, for their great
hospitality and support and for maintaining the rich heritage that has
nurtured their family's traditions.

In addition, we thank the people in the Chicano/Latino community in
Sacramento and La Raza Bookstore / Galería Posada for the Día de
Muertos mask workshop held there.

The public is welcome to participate in the Día de Muertos celebration
and procession in Sacramento. For more information about the celebration
or about the artist, Armando Cid, please contact:
La Raza Bookstore / Galería Posada
704 O Street
Sacramento, CA 95814
(916) 446-5133

About the Artist / Armando Cid

For more than twenty years, Día de Muertos has
been a major theme in the work of artist Armando
Cid. When he was a boy, he learned the art of
papier-mâché from his mother, who grew up in
Mexico. In preparation for family celebrations,
they made piñatas for parties, calaveras or paper
skulls for Día de Muertos, and small bowls
and animals for Las Posadas, a celebration at
Christmastime.

Today Armando Cid holds a masters degree
in Fine Art with an emphasis in printmaking
and sculpture. His work has been exhibited
in galleries and museums throughout the South-
west. Skeletons and calaveras animate the studio
space as Armando Cid creates new masks for the
Day of the Dead celebration. Three-dimensional
skeletons made of papier-mâché, some three or
four feet high, ride bicycles or seem to march in
a procession across the room. For Armando Cid,
these creations are a link between the present
and the Mexican traditions of the past.

Armando Cid is also a community activist and
organizer. He took part in the Chicano/Indio
Movement of the 1970s, a social effort designed
to give a voice to creative and political expressions
of Americans with a Mexican Indian heritage.
He became a co-founder of the Día de Muertos
Observance in Sacramento, California in 1974.
Armando Cid continues to create cultural
awareness and understanding through the
many workshops he conducts on the themes
of Mexican folklore, art, and traditions.

DAY OF THE DEAD
A Mexican-American Celebration

BY DIANE HOYT-GOLDSMITH

PHOTOGRAPHS BY LAWRENCE MIGDALE

HOLIDAY HOUSE ▪ NEW YORK

This book is dedicated
to all of our *antepasados*,
but especially to
Joe N. Talamantez,
our Yaqui grandfather

February 10, 1912 – November 1, 1992

Our names are Ximena *(chee-MEN-ah)* and Azucena *(ah-soo-SEN-nah)*. We are ten years old and live in Sacramento, California, with our parents. We have two brothers, Miguel *(mee-GEL)*, age eight, and Armando *(ar-MON-doh)*, age eleven. We also have an older sister named Zenaida *(zeh-NAY-dah)* who is thirteen. In our home, we speak Spanish as well as English, because we have many ties to Mexico where our father was born.

Azucena and Ximena are fraternal twins. They were born a few minutes apart, but they do not look exactly alike the way identical twins do.

Azucena gets ready to pitch a softball. Both twins enjoy sports and play on a team in the community.

We are twins. Although we don't look exactly alike, we enjoy doing a lot of the same things. Our favorite sports are softball and soccer. We both like to have slumber parties and listen to music. We are also artistic.

Our mother tells us that we get our creativity from our father, who is a professional artist. He makes a living by selling his sculptures, paintings, and prints. Our father's work is influenced by the traditional folk arts of Mexico. He specializes in making masks and large sculptures out of papier-mâché. For him, being creative is a part of everyday life.

Our mother is artistic, too. She enjoys dancing, creating masks, doing beadwork, making prints, and writing. She has a job with the California Arts Council. This government agency supports musicians, dancers, actors, and other artists who live and work in California. Our mother and her coworkers help artists create and present their work by providing them with financial support. Our mother enjoys collaborating with other people.

We like to work with people, also. We get together with some of the other students at school to do projects that improve life at school and in the community. Whether it is running for office in the Student Council, working on the school yearbook, or serving on a committee to organize a talent show, we like to work with other kids to get things done.

Our father was born in the state of Zacatecas *(sah-cah-TEK-kas)* in central Mexico. When he was just a baby, he and our grandparents moved to the United States. His father, our grandfather, was born in Nebraska, although his parents were Mexican. His family moved back to Mexico when he was a teen-ager. It was there that he met our grandmother and married.

Because our grandfather was born in the United States, he is a citizen of this country. When World War II started, he enlisted in the United States Army. While he was fighting in the war, the rest of the family, including our father, moved from Mexico to California.

Azucena and Ximena go downtown to visit their mother at work. Her office is located near the state capitol building in Sacramento.

Ximena and Azucena live a few blocks from their grandparents. They like to ride their bicycles to their grandparents' home.

Although Sacramento is far from our grandparents' original home, they kept the traditions of Mexico alive as they raised their six children. They speak Spanish at home and continue to celebrate the holidays and observe the customs of Mexico. Although they have lived in the United States for more than forty years, the special character of the Mexican culture touches every part of their lives.

When our grandparents first settled in Sacramento, other immigrants from Mexico were already living here. My grandparents joined a community that had strong cultural roots. They celebrated many of the festivals of Mexico. *Cinco de Mayo (SEEN-koh dah MY-oh)* is the day on which we remember Mexico's battle at Puebla against the French. The Sixteenth of September, called *Dieciséis de Septiembre (dee-ACE-ee-SES dee seh-tee-EM-brey)* in Spanish, celebrates Mexico's independence from Spain. Between December 19 and Christmas, we celebrate *Las Posadas (lahs poh-SAH-dahs)*. This festival re-creates Mary and Joseph's search for lodging in Bethlehem.

In 1974, our father helped to revive a celebration that was new to Sacramento but traditional to all the Mexican–Americans who lived there. He and other people in the community began to celebrate *Día de Muertos (DEE-ah dey MWER-tos)*, the Day of the Dead. This holiday takes place on the first and second day of November. We celebrate the Day of the Dead to honor all of our relatives and friends who have died during the year. The celebration has roots in the ancient history of Mexico, long before there was any contact with European cultures.

Helping their grandmother prepare a traditional recipe for rice called <u>arroz a la mexicana</u> (ah-ROHS ah lah meh-hee-CAHN-ah), Azucena and Ximena have a chance to learn about their heritage. The handmade platters, bowls, and <u>ollas</u> (OY-yahs) were collected by their grandmother and brought from Mexico.

9

Día de Muertos

The drawing of an ancient clay head found in Oaxaca (wah-HAWK-ah) shows both life and death. The left side of the face shows life, while on the right, it is a skeleton.

Many Mexican and Latin American people of Indian heritage believe that each year, on Día de Muertos, the souls of their departed relatives return to share a feast with the living.

Long before the Aztecs built a civilization in the Valley of Mexico, the people of Central America and Mexico held special ceremonies for the dead. Many of the Aztec gods, as well as their beliefs about the nature of life, developed out of vast urban civilizations that flourished and then disappeared over a period of several thousands of years. These ancient cultures developed throughout Mesoamerica, an area that includes most of central and southern Mexico, the countries of Belize and Guatemala, and parts of Honduras and El Salvador.

The Aztecs, who came into the Valley of Mexico in about 1325, inherited many traditions from these ancient cultures. They believed in a great number of different gods. There was a god of rain, a god of fire, a god of maize, and many others. For the Aztecs, every part of life was influenced by the actions of the gods.

For these people, the dead were an important part of the world of the living. People believed that spirits in the afterworld could influence what happened to them on earth and that the spirits could act as messengers to the gods.

For the Aztecs, the way a person died determined what kind of an afterlife he would have. When a person died a natural death, he entered *Mictlan (MEEK-tlan),* "the place of the dead," to embark upon a long and difficult journey through the nine levels of the underworld. During this time, the spirits of the dead would face many trials, such as fierce jaguars, mountains of dangerous heights, and winds as sharp as obsidian knives.

For the Aztecs, Mictlan had a real geography. It was much like the world of the living, with rivers and mountains. A dead person was buried with many useful objects for the long trip ahead. Household articles such as pots and pans, clothing, jewelry, food, and even toys were put into the grave with the corpse. All of these things were meant to help the spirit on its journey through the underworld.

People who died violently had a special fate. Rather than traveling to the underworld, the Aztecs believed that these spirits went directly to one of thirteen celestial levels in the heavens. Warriors, for example, who died in battle, went to a place in the sky where they traveled with the sun god, *Tonatiuh (TOH-nah-TEE-ooh),* on his daily journey across the sky.

Those who died by drowning went to a part of the heavens ruled by the rain god, *Tlaloc (tla-LOK).* This was a rain forest paradise. It was a pleasant place, full of green and yellow plants like maize, chilies, squash, tomatoes, beans, and marigolds. In this place called *Tlalocan (tla-lok-KAHN),* it was always springtime.

Babies and little children who died went to a place called *Chichihuacuauhco (chee-chee-hwa-KWAH-ooh-koh),* where an immense tree fed them by dripping milk from its branches.

These ancient beliefs developed into celebrations for the dead. The Aztec calendar divided the year into eighteen months, each with twenty days, and ending with five "useless," leftover days. During each month, festivals called *veintenas (vehn-TEH-nahs)* were held in honor of the gods.

These early veintenas gave rise to the celebrations of Día de Muertos or the Day of the Dead, a time for the spirits to return to visit their family and friends still living on earth. They came back to see that all was well and that they had not been forgotten. It was a time for the dead to feast on their favorite foods, to hear the music that once made them happy, and to be with the people they loved.

This mask, in the shape of a skull, is made of papier-mâché and painted with flower and plant designs. The skull or calavera (cah-lah-VER-ah) mask is usually worn in the Day of the Dead procession.

QUETZALCOATL
(ket-sahl-KWATL)
The Aztec god of the wind,
the Creator.

MICTLANTECUHTLI
(MEEK-tlan-teh-KOOT-lee)
The Aztec god of the underworld,
the god of Death

When the Spanish conquistadores arrived on the Mexican peninsula in the 1500s, they brought the Christian religion with them from Europe. The Spanish priests tried to stop the Indian celebrations of the dead, because these beliefs were different from Christian teachings. But the traditions of the Indian people were too strong.

It just so happened that the festivals for the little children who died, and the festival for the adults who died, came at the same time of year as the Catholic celebrations of All Saints' Day and All Souls' Day. So these Catholic traditions were combined with the veintenas. As a result, today there is a blending of ancient Indian customs with the religious beliefs of Catholic Christianity.

In ninth-century Europe, the celebration of All Saints' Day on November 1 was a time to honor the saints of the Catholic Church. In the thirteenth century, November 2 became All Souls' Day, a time to pray for the souls of the departed.

Beginning in the Middle Ages, All Hallows' Een was the eve of All Saints' Day. Over time it lost its religious significance and came to be called Halloween. So, although the Day of the Dead and Halloween occur at the same time of year, the two holidays come from very different traditions and origins.

There are plenty of skulls and skeletons on the Day of the Dead but they are not meant to be frightening. The skulls are painted bright colors and are often decorated with pretty flowers. These friendly skeleton faces remind us of the beliefs of our ancestors from the days of the Aztecs and before.

Many people in Central America and Mexico still think of death as a continuation of life. People believe that the spirit lives on after the body dies.

For the Aztecs, the gods of life and death were very powerful. Our father tells us a story about how the first Aztecs came to be. In the story, the ancient Aztec gods of life and death try to outsmart one another, but in the end, the god of life triumphs.

How the Aztecs Came to Be

Long, long ago, before jaguars walked the forest floor and quetzals hid high in the branches of the trees, all the people on the earth perished in a mighty flood. Their bones washed down to the underworld, where Mictlantecuhtli kept them locked away.

Quetzalcoatl, who could make the wind howl across the land, was lonely for company. He wanted to see men and women walk the earth once again. He liked their chattering voices, their gentle music, and the sweet sounds of children laughing.

He made a plan to get the bones of the people away from Mictlantecuhtli. He took Xolotl (show-LOTL), the dog god who was his faithful companion, with him.

Quetzalcoatl called out, "I have come for the precious bones that you keep here."

"Very well," Mictlantecuhtli replied. "Take my conch shell and blow upon it. If you can make it sound, you shall have the bones."

But the conch had no hole for the sound. So worms came to help Quetzalcoatl. They ate a hole into it, and bees and hornets flew inside. Their buzzing made it sound.

Mictlantecuhtli agreed to let Quetzalcoatl have all the bones. He said, "Go ahead and take them."

But then he changed his mind. He had the people of Mictlan dig a large pit. Quetzalcoatl stumbled into it, scattering the bones all around him as he fell. When Quetzalcoatl recovered, he gathered up the fragments, and bound them into a bundle.

He and Xolotl carried them to Tamoanchan (tah-moh-ahn-CHAN), where they were ground into a fine powder. Quetzalcoatl mixed some of his own blood with the bone dust to create a new race of men and women called the Aztecs. Because the bones were broken into pieces, some short and others long, the Aztec people appeared in many different sizes.

Miguel holds a basket of <u>pan de muertos</u> (PAHN day MWER-tos), or "bread of the dead." The loaves often are shaped like people and decorated with bright pink sugar. Traditionally, the dough is made without sugar, fat, or salt. This bread is usually included in the ofrenda.

The Celebration

The celebration of the Day of the Dead begins at home. Our whole family works together to create an altar in one corner of the dining room. The altar is a place of honor for the departed souls of our relatives. When they return for their yearly visit, they will find things on the altar that they remember—a photograph, a well-loved article of clothing, a hat, or perhaps a favorite shawl.

We call this altar an *ofrenda (oh-FREN-dah)* or offering. We offer food, fruits, flowers, clothing, and photographs in honor of the dead during their brief visit with us on earth.

We prepare traditional Mexican foods for the ofrenda. We like to make *tamales (tah-MAH-lays)*, a mixture of meat, spices, and cornmeal wrapped up in corn husks, and *mole (MOH-lay)*, a spicy sauce made from chocolate, nuts, and tomatoes. We offer a special drink made of corn called *atole (ah-TOH-lay)*.

To complete the celebration, people from the community go to the cemetery on November 1 to clean and fix up the graves of departed relatives. They place new flowers on the tombstones and light candles. In some parts of Mexico, a vigil is kept that lasts the whole night long. People feast near the graves of their loved ones, burning candles to light the darkness.

In Mexico, people save a part of their salary all year so they will have enough money to prepare a lavish feast and make a beautiful ofrenda. It is also traditional for people to buy or make new clothes for this festival.

In Sacramento, as in other parts of the United States, Mexican-American communities have found their own way of celebrating. Here we form a procession through the cemetery. Afterward, there is a Catholic Church service and a Mexican Indian ceremony.

The Ofrenda

During the last few weeks of October, we start to prepare for Día de los Muertos. Our family goes to the banks of the Sacramento River that flows through the city. We cut down several large reeds with a heavy knife called a *machete (mah-CHET-tey)*.

Ximena helps her father and her older brother Armando cut some reeds to make an arch for the ofrenda.

15

After the reed arch has been placed over the table in the corner of the dining room, the children unpack the decorations. The masks on the table and the skeleton figures in the background were all made by their father. He also created the portrait on the wall, a mixed-media silk-screen print of Frida Kahlo (FREE-dah KAH-loh), a well-known Mexican painter. Kahlo collected Día de Muertos objects.

When we get home with the reeds, our father ties them together to make the arch over the altar. Its shape represents a sacred opening. It frames the ofrenda that we make. We decorate the arch with real flowers and with blossoms made from bright-colored tissue paper.

Next we bring up the boxes from the basement that hold the holiday decorations we have been collecting over the years. We unwrap brightly painted masks, sparkling cut-glass bottles, the delicate feathered wing of a hawk, whistles, drums and other musical instruments, paper flowers, and much more. We have fun finding the treasures in the boxes. It is a little like unpacking the ornaments for our Christmas tree.

Each year we make something new to put on the altar. This year we made little cherubs, or angels, out of papier-mâché. We painted each angel in bright colors to go on the wall above the altar.

When it comes to making new things for the ofrenda, we are lucky that our father is a professional artist and teacher. He shows us how to create many special objects, like skeleton masks, toys, and even T-shirts. Although he makes things in the traditional way, using techniques he learned from his mother and other Mexican artists, he sometimes uses modern materials and methods as well.

This year, as we worked on making our ofrenda, we thought about our cousin, Ron Talamantez-Nevarez. In April, he died of AIDS. We miss him very much. He was only thirty-two years old and a special part of our family. We put his picture on our altar. Before he died, he gave our mother a small leather pouch called a "medicine bag." She put it on the altar in his memory.

Our mother says that the ofrenda is a serious space. "It is a remembering space," she tells us, "and a good place to do artwork." Our whole family works to make the ofrenda as beautiful and creative as possible. When it is finished, we are very proud.

The whole family works together to make the ofrenda beautiful. Ximena and Armando take time out to play the flutes, bells, and rattles that their parents have collected for the Day of the Dead celebration.

17

Burning incense made from sage and <u>copal</u> (coh-PAHL), a fragrant resin from a tree that grows in Mexico, is a traditional way to begin the construction of the ofrenda.

There are candles to light the way of the returning spirits, a bottle of orange soda to quench their thirst, corn and tamales, and pan de muertos. In the center, a sugar skull or <u>calavera</u> stares at life. On the Day of the Dead in Mexico, each child is given a little sugar skull, like this one—with his or her name written across the forehead in frosting.

When the ofrenda is finished, everyone in the family is proud. Ximena lights all the candles.

These characters were created by José Guadalupe Posada (poh-SAH-dah). La Catrina (lah kah-TREE-nah) (above) shows the bones of a woman from high society, still wearing an elegant hat. The figure of Madero (mah-DEHR-roh) (below) represents the man who became president of Mexico in 1911. In each of these engravings, perhaps Posada was saying that everyone, no matter how rich or famous, dies sooner or later.

The Masks

Masks are important to the celebration of the Day of the Dead. When we wear masks, our true identity is hidden. Traditionally, masks are worn during the procession in the cemetery and for acting in plays. They are also used to decorate the ofrendas.

Our skeleton masks are often funny. These images poke fun at death. We think about how Quetzalcoatl was able to fool Mictlantecuhtli, and we laugh. We aren't afraid to be around these masks. We have grown up with them. To us, they are like old friends.

Many papier-mâché masks of the skull or calaveras are inspired by the drawings of a Mexican artist who lived long ago. His name was José Guadalupe Posada (1851–1913). He illustrated booklets, songbooks, and posters with black-and-white drawings. Posada liked to use the image of the skeleton in his designs, creating humorous images of death. His characters are skeletons, but they are dressed in the latest styles. Posada's work was forgotten until the 1920s when he was rediscovered by artists like José Clemente Orozco, Diego Rivera, and contemporary Chicano artists like our father.

There are many ways to make a skeleton mask. Some techniques are very old and traditional. My father has several ceramic molds he created from clay and plaster. We use these as a base on which to build a skeleton's face. By layering strips of paper dipped in wheat paste, one on top of the other, we make a papier-mâché form.

After the papier-mâché has dried, we gently peel the mask away from the mold. The last thing we do is paint it. We start by painting the entire surface with one color, then add details and designs in other colors.

The whole family, including Grandma and Grandpa, helps to make new masks in the traditional papier-mâché style from Mexico. Clay or plaster molds are used as a base for making the skull masks called calaveras.

1 The twins' father gives a workshop in mask making at the La Raza Bookstore and Galería Posada in Sacramento. He teaches a modern technique using plaster casting materials. First he rubs Vaseline or vegetable oil onto the skin so that the plaster will not stick to it.

2 Azucena dips small strips of plaster and fabric in water to moisten them. Then Ximena applies them to her sister Zenaida's face, one by one.

3 Armando leaves openings for the nose and eyes.

4 As the plaster dries, the mask begins to get warm to the touch. A chemical reaction in the plaster gives off the heat. After the material cools, the plaster can be gently pried from the face.

5 The finished mask is quite sturdy when it is dry. The surface can be painted and decorated with glitter and pretty feathers.

A modern mask-making technique is to mold a mask on our own face. This method uses a material from which doctors make casts — gauze with plaster. First, we cover our face with Vaseline or vegetable oil to prevent the plaster from sticking to our skin. Then we cut small strips of the dry plaster fabric and dip them in water. We apply these wet plaster strips to the face, one by one, in overlapping strips.

We leave open spaces for the nose, the eyes, and sometimes the mouth. After a few minutes on the face, the plaster starts to heat up. This warmth means that a chemical reaction is starting and the plaster is getting hard. After a few more minutes, the mask can be pulled off.

Because it is modeled directly on the face, this mask fits perfectly — almost like a second skin. We paint the mask and decorate it with glitter, feathers, and spangles.

Wearing their masks, the children look like visitors from another world.

The family leaves for the cemetery wearing skeleton masks and special T-shirts for the Day of the Dead. They bring along skeleton figures made of papier-mâché to carry in the procession.

The Procession

The Mexican-American community in Sacramento gathers on the afternoon of November 2 in St. Mary's cemetery. All the people, both young and old, participate. Some wear brightly painted skeleton masks. Others come as living skeletons, painting their faces with white and black and wearing dark clothes. Still others pay tribute to their heritage and dress in traditional Mexican clothing.

As people gather outside the gates, the ceremony begins with a prayer for the dead. Starting in the north, everyone walks through the cemetery in a procession.

Many people burn incense. Our mother carries an incense burner called an *incensario (in-sen-SAHR-ee-oh)*. She explains that the copal is mixed with sage and sweet grass. This makes a sweet-smelling smoke that helps to carry our prayers to heaven. Our mother also carries a metal rattle, which she shakes loudly from time to time.

The procession is not a typical parade where people are having fun and showing off. People have come to be part of a community prayer, another ofrenda or offering for the dead. Here they remember and grieve together. The atmosphere is serious and many people cry as they think of those who have died.

After the opening prayers, the marchers visit each of the four directions: north, west, south, and east. Each direction is symbolic of a different group of the dead. The procession visits the north first, where a prayer is given for the elders, *los ancianos (los ahn-see-AHN-os)*. Here we think about grandparents or elderly friends who have died. This is also a time to say a prayer for our ancestors, for all the people who came before us.

(Top) People gather for the procession to walk and pray in honor of the dead. The twins help carry the arch from the family ofrenda.

(Right) Some marchers paint their faces black and white and dress in black robes to become living "skeletons."

25

Marchers carry wreaths in the procession through the cemetery. At each stopping place, people place a marigold blossom in the wreath to honor someone who has died.

Then the procession moves to the west. We stop and gather in a circle to honor *las mujeres (las moo-HEHR-es)*, all the women who have died. Here people who have lost a mother, a daughter, a sister, or a friend come forward one by one and place a marigold in a large wreath. As they say the dead person's name, the people in the crowd rattle their instruments loudly. Afterward, the crowd joins together to sing a song for the Virgin of Guadalupe, patron saint of Mexico. They sing, *"Santa María, madre de Dios ..."*

Marigolds have a special meaning in the celebration. In Mexico, this flower is called *cempasúchil (sem-pah-SOO-chil)* or "flower of the dead." Because these flowers have a strong fragrance, the petals are often strewn in a path from the cemetery to each house. People believe that the scent of the blossoms helps the spirits find their way back home.

Next the procession goes to the south. Here a prayer is given for the children and infants, *los angelitos (los ahn-hel-LEE-tos)* or little angels, who died before they had time to experience much of life. Again, mourners come forward to say the child's name and add a blossom to the wreath. There are many tears as people experience their grief once again.

The procession moves on to a section of the cemetery that has a monument dedicated to the people who have died in war. Several people speak about their sons, husbands, or brothers who were lost while serving their country. Even more blossoms are added to the wreath.

The procession continues. The final stopping point is in the east. Here we honor the men who have died, the warriors, *los guerreros (los gehr-RER-ros)*. People come forward to say the names of fathers, husbands, brothers, and sons. Many more marigold blossoms are added to the wreath.

The last stop is in the east because this is where the sun rises each morning. According to Aztec belief, this is also where the spirit first enters the body of Earth at birth.

(Top) At each point on the compass, north, west, south, and east, the community gathers in a circle to remember the dead. Prayers are recited and songs are sung.

(Right) The twins' father blows the conch shell, an ancient instrument whose mournful sound calls the spirits.

27

(Top) The procession moves through the cemetery, led by marchers carrying an image of the Virgin of Guadalupe.

(Left) In the east, Ximena steps up to place a blossom in the wreath in memory of her cousin Ron. At the end of the procession, the wreath is covered with marigolds.

At the end of the procession, there is a large ofrenda, built by the people in the community to honor all the dead. There are many photographs, foods, and decorations. Late in the afternoon, a priest from the Catholic church comes to perform a Mass in Spanish.

Then, as the sun sinks lower in the sky and evening approaches, the group gathers around the simple altar on the ground. This ofrenda is for all the forgotten ones. Here we honor the dead who have no family or friends to mourn them.

The pounding of Aztec drums begins, and dancers put on elaborate feathered headdresses. Some wear bells around their ankles that jingle with every step. Soon they begin to move to the ancient rhythms of old songs, dancing in a circle around the altar on the ground.

Our mother has come to the procession dressed in a native costume influenced by several Mexican Indian tribes — the Zapotec *(sah-POH-tec)*, Puebla *(PWEB-lah)*, and Yaqui *(YAH-kee)*. The Yaqui Indians, her father's people, have lived near the border between the United States and Mexico for many hundreds of years. Although our mother's heritage is Yaqui Indian, she grew up speaking Spanish.

Wearing a mask that she made herself, our mother joins the dancers in their traditional movements. Whirling, turning, and stamping her feet, she dances without shoes. She balances, sometimes on one foot, sometimes on the other, as she turns and turns and turns.

The dancing and the music are an important ending to the procession. The dancers' movements show their unity with the souls of the people who have lived before them and are now a part of the spirit world. The music, created by people thousands of years in the past, communicates a love of life that comes straight from the ancestral spirit world of long ago.

As daylight fades from the sky, our family leaves the cemetery to go back home. We stay up late and eat together. We tell stories about our relatives, celebrating our memories of them.

A Catholic priest performs a Mass for all the participants when the procession ends at the ofrenda made by the community.

29

(Left) Putting on a feathered headdress, the twins' mother gets ready to dance. This Mexican Indian tradition follows the Catholic Mass.

(Right) The dancers stay until nightfall, moving to the rhythm of ancient drums and music.

In life and in death, the Mexican-American community is strong partly because it stays together. Somehow it is comforting to think that we can come back after death, even if only for a short time each year, to visit the people who love and remember us.

As we celebrate the Day of the Dead, we are in touch with our ancient ancestors. The Aztec beliefs, though changed by time and history, are still an important part of our lives.

Glossary

ancianos, los: *(los ahn-see-AHN-os)* Spanish for "the elders."

angelitos, los: *(los ahn-hel-LEE-tos)* Spanish for "the little angels."

arroz a la mexicana: *(ah-ROHS ah lah meh-hee-CAHN-ah)* Mexican dish of rice made with onions.

atole: *(ah-TOH-lay)* A drink made from cornmeal.

Aztecs: The people of "Aztlan" from "the place of whiteness, the place of heroes" in the Nahuatl language. The Aztecs moved into the Valley of Mexico in A.D. 1325 and built a great civilization there. In 1521, the Aztecs were defeated by the Spanish and their civilization began to decline. However, the language, foods, and beliefs of the ancient Aztecs continue to influence the culture of modern-day Mexico.

cempasúchil: *(sem-pah-SOO-chil)* Nahuatl name for marigold, "flower of the dead," used in festivals for the dead since pre-Hispanic times.

chicano, chicana: Man or woman of Mexican heritage living in the United States.

Cinco de Mayo: *(SEEN-koh dah MY-oh)* Held on May 5, this festival celebrates the victory of Benito Juárez and the Mexican army over the French army at Puebla in 1862.

conquistadores: Soldiers from Spain sent to Mexico to conquer the population by force. Hernán Cortés landed in Mexico in 1519 and had conquered the Aztecs by 1521.

Cortés, Hernán: *(kawr-TEHZ, ehr-NAHN)* (1485–1547) A Spanish conquistador whose military triumphs over the Indians in central and southern Mexico led to Spanish rule of the area for three centuries.

Dieciséis de Septiembre: *(dee-ACE-ee-SES dee seh-tee-EM-brey)* Mexican Independence Day, held on September 16, celebrates the end of 300 years of Spanish rule.

guerreros, los: *(gehr-RER-ros, los)* Spanish for "the warriors."

Mictlan: *(MEEK-tlan)* The land of the dead in Aztec mythology.

Mictlantecuhtli: *(MEEK-tlan-teh-KOOT-lee)* The god of death and the underworld in Aztec mythology.

mole: *(MOH-lay)* A spicy sauce in Mexican cooking that includes the ingredient chocolate.

mujeres, las: *(moo-HEHR-es, las)* Spanish for "the women."

Nahuatl: *(NAH-wahtl)* The language of the Aztecs.

ollas: *(OY-yahs)* Handmade pottery vessels used for cooking, serving, and storing food.

Orozco, José Clemente: *(oh-ROHS-koh, ho-SEY kle-MEN-teh)* (1883–1949) A Mexican painter who became well known for large murals on the themes of Mexican history and mythology.

pan de muertos: *(PAHN day MWER-tos)* "Bread of the dead," baked in human shapes and decorated with pink sugar.

Posada, José Guadalupe: *(poh-SAH-dah, hoh-SEY GWA-dah-LOO-pay)* (1851–1913) A Mexican artist noted for graphic images of skeletons.

Posadas, Las: *(poh-SAH-dahs, las)* Celebrated from December 19 until December 24, this holiday re-creates Mary and Joseph's search for lodging in Bethlehem. Posada means "inn" or "shelter" in Spanish.

Quetzalcoatl: *(ket-sahl-KWATL)* The Aztec god of the wind and creation, usually pictured as half serpent and half quetzal bird.

Rivera, Diego: *(ree-VEHR-ah, dee-AY-goh)* (1886–1957) A Mexican artist known for many large murals showing the life and history of Mexico.

tamales: *(tah-MAH-lays)* A Mexican dish made of a mixture of meat and cornmeal that is wrapped in the husks of corn and then boiled.

Tamoanchan: *(tah-moh-ahn-CHAN)* The mythical site of the creation of humans.

Tlaloc: *(tlah-LOK)* The Aztec god of rain and lightning.

Tlalocan: *(tlah-lok-KAHN)* The mythical land of the god of rain.

veintenas: *(vehn-TEH-nahs)* Festivals to honor the gods, held during each month of the Aztec calendar.

Xolotl: *(show-LOTL)* The dog god of the Aztecs.

Yaqui: *(YAH-kee)* Indian people who now live in southern Arizona but were originally located in Sonora, Mexico.

Index

Numbers in italics refer to pages with photos.